Scary Ghost Stories

REAL Eyewitness Accounts: The World's Most Possessed Woods, Houses and Haunted Places

Table of Contents

Like books?

Would you like them delivered to you every week?

Do you like non-fiction books on a huge range of different topics?

We send out e-books every week so we can share our books with the world!

We have books every week on **AMAZON** that we send to our email list.

So if you want in, then visit the link at the end of this book to sign up and sit back and wait for new books to be sent straight to your inbox!

Introduction

What would you do if you ever encountered a spirit or otherworldly entity? Do you think you would flee the scene, screaming as you put as much distance between you and the unknown?

Or would you try your hardest to communicate with the entity?

The idea of ghosts and spirits is not a new concept. Records of ghosts have been reported since the beginnings of civilization as we know it.

But nothing prepares you for the moment you eventually come face to face with a paranormal entity.

This book covers many houses, public places and forests that are said to be the homes of the supernatural. In these places, the spirits are not shy in the presence of the living. Often they will whisper in a person's ear or touch the small of their back with their unseen, freezing fingertips. These spirits recollect fragments of their previous life—moments in which they too had been alive and well.

When exploring haunted locations, it is imperative to understand the nature of the haunting of each place. What had it been used for in the past? Did those who died in the house have a chance to say a proper goodbye to the world? Was their death peaceful? Or was it incredibly violent?

Each haunted location in our world has a unique background—a context in which to approach each marvelously haunted place. Sometimes the world is cruel and will steal a young life, or make a person endure a brutal and painful death. It is important to understand why certain spirits we encounter in specific places may seem angry or upset, and we must interact with them in a manner that reflects our understanding of the life they had lived...

The information herein is offered for informational purposes solely, and is universal as so. The presentation of the information is without contract or any type of guarantee assurance.

The trademarks that are used are without any consent, and the publication of the trademark is without permission or backing by the trademark owner. All trademarks and brands within this book are for clarifying purposes only and are the owned by the owners themselves, not affiliated with this document.

Chapter 1:
A Most Infamous Femme Fatale

In 1942, Louisiana passed a historical milestone: they executed their first female prisoner of the state. But Annie McQuiston, better known by her pseudonym Toni Jo, was famous before she met her maker in the electric chair. Her story feels like its straight out of a crazy Western film, filled with violence, crime and a cowboy to boot.

After the death of her mother, young Annie went to live with her aunt in Lake Charles. As Annie grew from childhood into a young teen, she began to realize that her welfare and future were of little or no consequence to her aunt. She decided that her life would be more fulfilling if she headed out on her own. Annie ran away from her home at the ripe age of thirteen.

With minimal education, Annie found it extremely difficult to find a respectable employer. Out of options, Annie found herself applying to become a prostitute at the local brothel. Within a short period of time, not only did Annie develop a less than respectable reputation around town, but she also became addicted to cocaine. Many believe it was during this point that Annie became known as Toni Jo.

Toni's life became entirely void of comfort and safety. No longer part of the moral society in Lake Charles, Toni Jo began to drift around the state - and often found herself at the wrong end of the law. She was charged with larceny, aggression and violence, not to mention vagrancy on numerous occasions.

It seemed that Toni Jo was destined for a life of debauchery, drug addiction, and disappointed hopes...that is, until she met her soul mate.

Enter Claude Henry...

One spring day in 1939, Texas native Claude, better known in his hometown as Cowboy, happened to enter the brothel Toni Jo found herself employed in at the age of twenty-three. The two met and quickly became inseparable. Toni Jo was in love like she had never been before. Claude was also smitten, and tried his best to be a positive influence on Toni. With love and encouragement, Claude even managed to rid Toni of her addiction to cocaine.

Both realized they never wanted to be apart. Shortly after they met, Claude and Toni were married. After a whirlwind honeymoon in sunny California, Toni wanted to return with her new beau to her hometown of Lake Charles, Louisiana.

But the moment they crossed the border, the honeymoon came to an abrupt halt. Minutes into being in Louisiana, local police had located Claude and arrested him. Unbeknownst to Toni, her new husband had gotten into a serious altercation with a police officer in Texas shortly before meeting her.

Claude wound up murdering the police officer, whether intentionally or accidentally. Rather than turn himself in, Claude had fled the scene of the crime. As a consequence, he became a fugitive. The moment Louisiana police arrested him, Claude was sent back to Texas to await a criminal trial.

Toni Jo was forced to endure watching her brand new husband be found guilty of the crime and sentenced to fifty years in prison, which would be served at the state penitentiary in Huntsville.

Now directionless and without her love, Toni Jo felt she had no other choice but to resume a life of prostitution. Her life in Louisiana was riddled with despair, drug use, and a desperate desire to see Claude once more. It wasn't long into their separation that Toni Jo hatched a notorious and dangerous scheme.

Convinced that the only way she could be reunited with her husband would be to get him out of jail, Toni decided to hire an accomplice, travel to Texas and break Claude out of the Texas State Penitentiary. Harold "Arkie" Burks agreed to accompany her and rescue Claude.

Arkie and Toni began their journey by hitch hiking their way out of Lake Charles. They met a man named Joseph Calloway who offered to give them a ride. As the two climbed into Joseph's V8 Ford Coupe, they realized that Calloway could do more than just give them a free ride - he could provide the perfect car in which to flee with Claude.

The two conspired together as they lounged in the backseat. When they approached a small town called Jennings, they asked if Joseph could pull off to the side of the road for a moment. After he did so, Arkie ordered the man out of his car. The dynamic duo forced Joseph to strip, and began to beat and torture him. After a while Toni reached back into the car and pulled out a pistol.

Toni instructed Joseph to say his prayers, then immediately shot him in the forehead. Joseph was dead within seconds. They rolled his naked body into the bushes at the side of the road and took off in the coupe, congratulating themselves on a job well done.

Successfully killing Joseph must have gone to their heads, because the moment they started to drink at a local bar, they began to boost about what they had done to some of the locals.

It didn't take long for the police to catch up with the pair of them and arrest them. Claude would have to remain in prison after all.

Arkie and Toni Jo were taken to Calcasieu Parish Courthouse for their hearings. Both took turns blaming the other for Joseph's murder. The court took it upon itself to find both guilty of the crime. Toni Jo was sentenced to death in March of 1940.

During the two years that Toni Jo remained in prison, she was given special treatment, such as being able to visit Claude on a somewhat regular basis. During one of those said visits, Toni Jo admitted to her husband that it was she who had murdered Joseph.

Toni's lawyers managed to get two additional trials for her, but each time the court found her to be guilty of the crime. Finally, November 28 1942 rolled around - the date of Toni Jo's execution. Toni believed she would be hanged to death, but during her time in prison, the state of Louisiana had changed its method of execution. Toni was sent to the electric chair instead.

Despite a failed escape attempt, Claude was given permission to say goodbye to his wife before her death. Toni Jo also wrote a letter to the court, clearing Arkie of the murder. However, Arkie was still sent to the electric chair.

Ironic Fates

After Toni Jo's execution, the Calcasieu Parish Courthouse became a site of paranormal activity. Most people believe it is the spirit of Toni Jo, as the hauntings did not begin until shortly after her death.

Several employees have reported hearing disembodied footsteps throughout the courthouse. Others have also experienced smelling perfume that none of the females in the office wear. Once in a while, Toni Jo will attempt to speak to people as they go about their daily work. A few have reported hearing her disembodied screams emanating from the area where she was executed.

Ironically, Claude was released from prison a few years later...

Chapter 2:
Suicide in the Trees.

Haunted forests are creepy enough as it is, but what about a forest that is haunted by the souls of people who committed suicide? The Aokigahara is a large, dense forest located in Japan. Hundreds of people have selected this particular forest as the ideal place to end their life. It seems that with each passing year, the forest becomes more and more haunted.

Over five hundred people have taken their own lives in Aokigahara since the 1950s. Sometimes called "The Suicide Forest," Aokigahara is now considered to be the second most haunted place in the entire world.

Japan has a long standing history of suicides. While today, many people around the globe consider committing suicide due to suffering from a fatal disease, drug addiction or severe chronic depression. However, Japanese culture considers suicide from a completely different perspective—one that stems from shame.

Most Japanese citizens have high expectations of themselves and of their family members. It is imperative that they succeed in honoring their family. Some contemplate and carry out suicide attempts when they feel they could not provide what they believed they should. In essence, many suicides that occur in Japan are based in giving into a specific kind of pressure one feels in their personal or professional life.

Today, Japan's government has posted signs scattered throughout the forest, begging visitors to reconsider the value of their life. Despite localized efforts, the Aokigahara continues to be a popular place for suicides.

And the combination of lost souls and suicidal spirits has made the Aokigahara incredibly haunted...

The Access Point of Hell?

Many believe that the Aokigahara became increasingly haunted due to the number of suicides committed there. However, some believe the forest was haunted long before that.

During harsh seasons throughout our history, there has often been times when there was not enough food to nourish everyone in one's family. When things were that bad, most families felt no choice but to abandon one of the family members.

This was often done by sending them into the nearest forest, in which they succumbed to hypothermia, starvation, and dehydration. Some locals believe this occurred at Aokigahara as well.

Now, apparitions are often seen, wandering between the trees of this intense forest. Some visitors have seen these spirits with the naked eye. They resemble a misty white form, hovering amongst the foliage.

Some Japanese citizens are convinced that the Aokigahara is a portal into Hell. They believe that the forest is where demons roam, luring people into committing suicide.

It is small wonder that many people refuse to enter the forest altogether. They believe it is not safe for their souls. Given what occurs in the forest on an almost daily basis, one can hardly blame them...

Chapter 3:
The Never-ending House of Ghosts

This story begins in Connecticut in the autumn of 1839 with a well to do family in New Haven, named The Pardees. Not long after Leonard and Sarah were married, they were expecting their first child. They had a daughter on that fateful day in September.

They named her Sarah, after her mother. As the years passed and Sarah grew older she became more and more beautiful. She caught the eye of a young gentleman in town named William Winchester. The Winchester family owned a promising t-shirt manufacturing business.

The two were soon married. Wanting to provide for his beautiful new bride, William invented the Volcanic Repeater, a rifle that could be reloaded by a lever, rather than by hand. He went on to improve upon his design and wound up creating the Henry Rifle.

It was incredibly ingenious at the time, as this gun can be reloaded after just three seconds between shots.

In 1866, the two realized they were going to have a baby. Sarah was overjoyed at the news. On July 15, their daughter, Annie, was born. Alas, it was not meant to be. Annie was diagnosed with marasmus, a disease in which the muscles quickly deteriorate. Annie died not long after being born.

Sarah was devastated, but not free from more tragedy. On March 7, 1881 William died of tuberculosis. Sarah was left with nothing more than a large control over the Winchester Company, as well as an inheritance of 20 million dollars.

Life After Death

Despite the fortune, Sarah was stricken with grief. She had lost both her daughter and her husband in a relatively short time span. When she failed to get better, a friend suggested that Sarah talk to a medium. Perhaps her knowledge of the other side could provide help for Sarah.

Sarah did seek out a medium, and the medium told her that William was present and had something he needed to tell her. The alleged spirit of William told Sarah that his family was cursed. As a result, Sarah had to endure the death of her husband and child...before she would find her own.

Frightened, Sarah wanted to know why the family was cursed. The medium communicated to her that the Winchesters were being haunted by the spirits of those who had died because of William's new line of guns.

When Sarah sought advice from the medium, the woman told her that in order to be safe from the spirits, Sarah would have to move to the west side of the United States, and that no matter what she did, she was never to stop building onto the house she purchased. If Sarah ever stopped the improvements, the medium was convinced the spirits would find her and claim her.

Thus, Sarah sold all of her belongings, and headed west, all the way to Santa Clara Valley, California. When she arrived she began to look for a home to purchase. When Sarah stumbled upon a six bedroom home under construction, she felt it was the perfect setting.

For the next thirty-six years, Sarah never stopped making improvements to the house, and adding additions. Many architectural oddities became part of the house's never-ending expansion. There are some staircases that go nowhere, fake closets, and chimneys that don't reach the roof.

As the house continued to expand, it became less and less cohesive. Soon, one could easily get lost in the labyrinth of the house. But this only added to Sarah's sense of comfort. She thought the house's confusing layout would make her that much harder for the spirits to find her.

In 1922 Sarah held a séance with the spirit in the house. Nobody is quite sure what transpired, but Sarah went to sleep that night and did not wake in the morning. Her (now rather small) fortune was left to a relative, and her house was sold to an investor.

Said investor took one look at the bizarre house and knew he wanted to open up an attraction there, in honor of Sarah and her strange abode. To this day nobody is quite sure how many rooms the house had. Some argue it was around 160, but anytime someone attempts to recount the rooms, they always lose track.

The Spirits Never Sleep

Now, many people in the area are convinced that Sarah, along with several other spirits, still linger at her house. Many of those who have visited the Winchester House have reported hearing disembodied voices and noises scattered throughout the property.

Scarier even than the windows opening and closing of their own accord, was the sudden influx of reports of apparitions seen in the house. They were always shadows, lingering at the corners of one's eye.

A couple of maintenance workers on the site claim that the spirits of carpenters linger at the house, and can be seen trying to fix up rooms. One caretaker said he heard a phantom spirit remove a phantom screw from the wall, and heard the ghost walk off into another room.

A colleague of his claimed he was the target of pranks pulled by some of the spirits of the house. He would lock the door of the house and look away for a moment, only to find that the door was somehow unlocked again.

On another occasion he turned off the lights in the house and went to leave. As the employee approached his car he looked back at the house to find that all of the lights on the third floor were back on...

It would seem to many people that a lot of spirits have stayed behind to reside at Winchester House in the afterlife. Several guests have reported smelling soup and other fare emanating from one of the many kitchens on site. Afterward they said they believed it was spirits, people who once cooked for Sarah when she was alive.

One of the house's many guests considers himself to be a sensitive. He informed fellow guests and their tour guide that he saw a violent act take place in the hayloft of the property. He witnessed a fight between two grown men. One attacked the other with a small, sharp object, and the wounded man died before the following morning.

One of the house tour guides also experienced an odd paranormal encounter. While she spoke to the guests that were accompanying her through the house, she kept hearing someone call her name. Except that no one had. One of the spirits of the house had communicated with her directly in her mind...

Tour guides and guests alike have reported seeing a specter in the basement, wearing overalls and a thick mustache. This spirit has been seen pushing a wheelbarrow along the floor. All of these spirits, besides Sarah, continue to work on the house throughout the afterlife, it seems.

Sarah herself has been spotted on occasion. Usually seen wearing a classic Victorian style gown, Sarah has been seen standing in the dining room, as employees have come into the room...

Chapter 4:
Land of the Demonic Children

Homes that become haunted by ghosts or poltergeists are rare, but are not altogether unheard of. Whether the house went through some level of renovation, or a loved one recently passed, many people have claimed to have seen or experienced paranormal activity within their home.

But what if the thing you encountered was a demon? What if a demon resided in your house and it wanted nothing more than to claim you for its own...

That is what happened to Latoya Ammons and her family one summer in Indiana. It began with small things, and grew steadily worse, as many hauntings are prone to do. Latoya began hearing strange voices from inside her home.

When the sounds persisted, Latoya decided to seek out a psychologist. She contacted Dr. Geoffrey Onyeuku and told him what was happening in her house.

The doctor at first believed that Latoya was suffering from hallucinations. But Latoya began opening up about other strange things that had happened...

Her sons started to act out. They would often growl, and take turns trying to choke one another. On one occasion when they saw their grandmother they went up to her and smashed their heads into hers. Latoya then told Geoffrey about the incident with the closet...

At one point she was in the house when she went looking for her son. She found him in the closet, in what appeared to be the middle of a very intense conversation. Latoya didn't see anybody, and thus she asked her son who he had been talking to. The son answered that there was someone in there who couldn't be seen. This invisible force had been telling him what it felt like to be killed.

Puzzled, Geoffrey asked to meet the children and see these things for himself. After extensive study, the psychologist admitted that the children were exhibiting behaviors he could not readily explain.

Child Services became involved with the case, and had two more crazy experiences to share with the doctor. One of the case workers witnessed one of the children being thrown into a wall when no one else was around. Another employee saw one of the other children walking up the wall backward. The case grew more baffling and terrifying by the minute.

The children were temporarily removed from Latoya's care, in order to confirm it was not a matter of domestic abuse. When she was cleared from suspicion, the children were returned to her, and the Ammons family quickly moved out of their house.

Fleeing the Demons

Tenants have come and gone from the house, and none of them have reported experiencing anything strange or unusual within the dwelling.

However, locals who knows Latoya's story are still rather convinced the house is a gateway into the underworld. Many skeptics who were involved with the case wound up believing in spirits when all was said and done. When psychics came around to visit the house they said it was the home of over two hundred demons...

Chapter 5:
The Many Anomalies of Epping Forest

This large forest, located in Essex, England, has become quite infamous over the years. The Epping is now shrouded in history and legend, and remains an elusive mystery to this day.

According to local rumors, the forest was once the regular meeting place for a young couple who lived in the area. One day the couple had stumbled upon a pool. As the girl's father did not approve of their relationship, the two would meet by the pool in secret to be together.

One night, the girl and her lover met by the pool, but they were suddenly interrupted by the girl's father who had followed them there from their house. Overcome with rage, the girl's father murdered her on the spot.

Unable to move on, the girl's lover visited the exact same location by the pool, and eventually committed suicide. According to the legend, after his death the pool turned black, and wildlife know not to drink from it.

The little pond is now known as suicide pool, and would likely have many visitors each year...if anybody ever managed to find it...

Historically speaking, Epping Forest was the home and hideout for infamous highway man Dick Turpin. Dick, accompanied by his partner in crime, Tom King, would lurk by the edge of the forest until travelers came down the road.

Leaping out of the trees, he would hold the passersby at gunpoint and demand their belongings. They would then disappear back into the woods, where they had made their private hideout. After Dick Turpin's death, his spirit is said to haunt the woods, keeping track of his fortune...

Other parts of Epping Forest have an even more sinister background. Due to its close proximity to London, a part of the forest was used to bury people who had been murdered in the city. Today, some of their ghosts are said to wander in the woods during the night.

Another portion of the forest, known as Hangman's Hill, is considered a paranormal anomaly. Many spook hills, or gravity hills, exist throughout the United States. These hills serve as an optical illusion due to the surrounding terrain. When it appears that a car is going up one of these hills, it is actually going downward. Many folks believed Hangman's Hill was one of these gravity hills because cars could move by themselves while on the hill.

As it turned out, the hill has been tested....and it isn't a gravity hill at all...

Chapter 6:
A Demon in the Smurl House

This tale begins in 1972, when Hurricane Agnes struck the east coast of the United States of America. Most of the area was flooded, and several families lost their homes in the extensive damage. Janet and Jack Smurl were victims of the storm. In 1973 they left their permanently damaged home and relocated to Pennsylvania.

They purchased a duplex, where Jack and Janet lived on one side, and Jack's parents, John and Mary, lived on the other. And for the first year, all appeared to be well. But by 1974, strange things began to happen...

Shocking and bizarre things started to take place, such as the television set suddenly catching on fire, or how their carpets began to be stained for no apparent reason. There were strange things going on in the house, but nothing that could not be explained away by shoddy workmanship or ordinary wear and tear.

Until the Activity Escalated...

But things not only continued - they got worse. Jack and Janet began to hear disembodied feet walking around the house. Cabinet doors began to open and close by themselves, and the radio would turn on, despite not being plugged in. And all of these events seem to be accompanied by a horrible sour smell.

John and Mary experienced a strange event of their own next door. One day they were both inside their part of the duplex when they heard two angry voices burst forth from behind the wall next door. Mary described the voices as being very loud and very foul mouthed.

When things seemed as though they could not get any worse, they did. Both Jack and Janet began to be violated sexually at night. This happened quite often.

The final straw for Janet was seeing a shadowy figure in the shape of a man in her house one day. Janet had walked into the kitchen just in time to see the manifestation walk through the wall and into John and Mary's side of the complex. Jack's parents had also seen the apparition and were positively horrified by it...

By then it was 1985, and the Smurl family realized they needed help. They contacted Ed and Lorraine Warren, who were well-known paranormal experts at the time. Ed and Lorraine visited the house and realized that it was under the control of three spirits and one demon.

When Ed and Lorraine failed to remove the demon by using holy water, the demon became angry. It started to shake mirrors on the walls, and shake drawers as well.

Soon the Smurls began to find bite marks and large cuts on their arms. The family decided to contact the Catholic Church and pleaded for assistance. However, the Church ignored their request...

Desperate for help, Ed and Lorraine brought in Father McKenna, a priest and friend of theirs, who proceeded to perform two exorcisms on the house. When both of these rites failed, the demon seemed to grow stronger and angrier...

The demon began to follow Jack to work – and even went on their family vacation...

Since the Church did not recognize their need for help, the Smurl family decided it was time for another desperate action – they invited the media into their home.

After being interviewed for a television show, entitled *The People are Talking,* the house became a tourist location. Everyone wanted to visit the haunted house and see with their own eyes what dwelled within.

When this invitation to the media failed to grant them help, the demon grew even more wrathful. He raped Jack as punishment for the deed.

The Smurl family wound up being haunted for a total of thirteen years before the Church finally put an end to it. The Scranton Diocese eventually became interested in the case, and allowed Father McKenna to continue. McKenna was able to dispel the demon, but it returned three months later.

At last, in 1988, the Catholic Church finally recognized the problem at the Smurl residence and performed a sanctioned exorcism. Thankfully, the ritual worked.

The 1991 film, *The Haunted,* was made about the Smurl House Demon...

Chapter 7:
Black Magic Women

Marie Laveau and her daughter, known as Marie II, lived in New Orleans, and would forever shape part of the city's culture. The mother daughter duo became known for practicing a unique blend of voodoo with a touch of Catholicism in it.

Everybody hailed them as "the most famous and powerful voodoo Queens of North America." Both mother and daughter were respected for their powers in their own right. Both answered the deepest desires of locals.

Some wanted fortune, some wanted fame, others wanted children or revenge. No matter what the customer wished, Marie and Marie II provided...

It all began when Marie I was born in 1794. She was of mixed parentage, which meant that Charles Laveaux, the plantation owner, had had an affair with his African American mistress, Margueritte Darcantrel. Marie I was born, and was raised in the household.

In 1819, Marie I married Jacques Paris, a Haitian man. But soon after their marriage, Marie I woke up one day to find her husband was no longer there. Some theorized that he had moved back to Haiti, while others speculated that he was dead. After five years of silence, Jacques was officially declared a dead man.

Marie I began to work as a hairdresser to make ends meet after her husband's disappearance. As she pampered women about town, they began to open up to Marie about the inner workings of their lives, their problems, and their deepest desires. During this time, Marie started to become interested in Voodoo.

In 1826, Marie I married Christophe Duminy de Glapion, another Haitian man. After the couple had fifteen children together, Marie I retired as a hairdresser. Instead, she raised the children and began to delve deeper into the world of voodoo...

The Merging of Religions

Voodoo became a popular, albeit discrete, practice in New Orleans when slaves began to arrive in the city. Catholicism was the dominating religion at the time, so voodoo went underground. Rumor began to spread of secret powers, and strange rituals...

Soon black slaves were practicing their arts, and slave owners began to worry an uprising maybe near. Soon, groups of white people began to join in these rituals, making the slave owners even more frightened.

The government eventually stepped in and said that black people could only gather together on Sundays and in a specific location only. They were allowed to gather in Congo Square, now known as Armstrong Park.

By 1830, Marie I had already developed a reputation for being very skilled in the art of voodoo. On most Sundays she led the dances at Congo Square. People began to line up to purchase one of her spelled amulets.

Marie I became known as Mamzelle, and became even more popular when she incorporated elements of Catholicism into her rituals. Mamzelle incorporated holy water, saint statutes, and Catholic prayers into each ceremony.

When white people asked to be a part of the group, she figured she could make a good profit off it. She agreed - if they paid a fee. Her popularity continued to grow, and she catered for many services - white men in particular.

Mamzelle began to seek out other financial opportunities to utilize her voodoo skills. She began to influence local judges, and insist they needed to pay for her services in order to win. Each candidate paid Mamzelle around a thousand dollars, which is equivalent to $25,000 today. She was also making a tidy profit on the side, selling powders for ten dollars ($250 now).

Rumors and stories spread about Mamzelle and her powers. Marie I never denied any of these stories, even the ones that seemed unlikely to be true. She knew the more popular she was, the better business would be.

In 1869, 70 year old Mamzelle declared she would be retiring. Marie I spent her life giving private readings, and visiting the poor.

When Marie I died seventeen years later, people were naturally shocked to see her walking around shortly after. The townsfolk began to speculate that Marie I was immortal when they discovered that the woman was not Mamzelle, but in fact, her daughter.

Marie II was born in February of 1827. After she grew up, she not only followed her mother in appearance, she also followed her in career paths. Marie II became a hairdresser.

After doing this for a few years, Marie II grew restless and sought out a new challenge. She decided to manage a bar and brothel instead. When Marie I passed on, Marie II was ready to adopt her role as Queen of voodoo. She managed Marie I's business ventures, and various schemes.

While Marie II carried the same demand for respect as her mother, she was feared more than loved, unlike Marie II. However, Marie II's reign did not last very long. She reportedly drowned in Lake Portchartrain during a severe thunderstorm.

Today, the mother and daughter duo are buried right beside each other in the St. Louise Cemetery. Their tombs are numbers 1 and 2 in the burial park. Their locations have become a prominent place for visitors, seeking the voodoo Queens to help them achieve their goals.

The Voodoo Queens... Reunited

St. Louise is considered to be one of the various haunted paces within New Orleans. Many visitors believe the spirit they most often see in the cemetery is in fact Marie I.

One gentleman claims to have fallen asleep against a tree while on a tour of the cemetery. When he awoke it was in the dark of night and he heard the sounds of drums and chanting. Following the sound, he found a series of naked ghosts dancing upon Marie I's tomb. With them was a enchanting woman who had a snake wrapped around her body. This iconic snake made the visitor realize he was witnessing the spirit of Marie I.

Elmore Lee Banks, a local African American man, was inside the resident pharmacy when an old woman walked into the store. The shop owner took one look at the woman and shrieked in fright, and retreated into the offices at the rear of the building.

The woman then proceeded to approach Elmore and demanded to know if he knew who she was. When Elmore replied that no, he did not, the woman seemed to become angry at his honesty. She struck him across the face, then seemed to glide through the wall and back into the cemetery in a matter of seconds...

Elmore was so overcome with shock, he fainted. When he finally revived, the shop owner told him the woman had been Marie I. Both fear and awe of this woman still radiates throughout New Orleans. You just never know when you might run into her on the street...

Chapter 8:
In the Land of Possessed Dolls

There have been enough horror stories and scary movies about dolls to make them high on the list of things people tend to fear. Given the right appearance, expression and back story, dolls can be downright terrifying.

Now imagine a whole island of them...

The island La Isla de la Munecas is located near Mexico City. Situated near the center of Lake Teshuilo, the island is the center of a local story. Many people say that during the 1950s, three little girls were playing by the shoreline when one of the girls fell in. The girl tried to swim, but she drowned.

Not long after this occurrence the island was purchase by a man named Julian Santan Barrera. He moved to the island and was visited by the dead girl. She told him about the final moments of her death, and told him that she was trapped on the island...

Julian was scared but also sympathetic. Since she was forever trapped on the island, Julian went out and bought her a couple of dolls to play with. The ghost girl was delighted - and wanted more. With every passing year she required more and more dolls to be appeased.

The girl had grown quite fond of Julian and began to demand that he join her in death. Julian began to fear for his life and contacted his nephew. His nephew knew about the girl on the island and set out to help his uncle.

But when he arrived at the island he found Julian face down in the water, right where the girl had once drowned...

The Scariest Island Ever

Today, La Isla de la Munecas is covered in dolls attached to trees, ropes and buildings. Locals are convinced that the dolls possess the spirit of the little girl in them, and move of their own accord. Sometimes they can even be heard whispering to each other through the night.

A few paranormal investigators have even visited this island and have found it to be a chilling and supernatural experience to behold.

So if you have a fear of dolls, and want to challenge yourself, plan a visit to Lake Teshuilo. See for yourself if the dolls on the island move their heads to watch you as you walk by...

Chapter 9:
The Voices in the Forest

Pluckley, a little sleepy town in Britain, is known to be quite a haunted village. South of the town is Dering Woods, or what locals refer to as the Screaming Woods.

The nickname was derived on account of two spirits that live in the woods. One is said to be a highwayman who used to rob travellers that traveled beside the Dering Woods. The highwayman was eventually caught by a handful of villagers. As punishment for his crimes, the man was tied up to a tree and run through with a sword.

As the man began to die, he cried out at the pain of it.

Another spirit is that of a man who fell to his death within the woods. Legend has it that as he fell, he screamed the entire way down...

As the years went by, the Dering Woods became quite popular. A group of friends was traveling through the town when they decided to stop in Pluckley and explore the infamous forest.

One of the group members took notice of the birds singing above them in the treetops, and everything felt light and carefree. But as they got closer to the borderline, the atmosphere took a turn for the worse. Each group member took note that the birds were no longer singing - in fact the silence was positively deafening...

The group had heard that it was important to locate the crossroads if they wished to see one of the spirits. The group made it halfway there when the females in the group decided to turn back and head toward the cars.

The males carried on. After the girls got back into the vehicles, they saw the boys running back their way, looking quite panicked. The group were quickly reassembled within the cars, and they each struggled to start their cars despite shaky hands.

One of the cars stalled and that is when every member of the group peered out their windshields and saw a black form walking down the path toward them. They got the car started, and the group sped off in fright.

Later, when they discussed their paranormal adventure in the woods with folks at the local pub, nobody seemed particularly surprised that they had such a crazy experience. Many of the townspeople hear the screams each night, and know better than most that the Dering Woods is haunted...

Chapter 10:
Where the Devil Most Roams

Stull, Kansas is home to a location that has been called many names, including Satan's Burial Ground, and the Seventh Gate to Hell.

Over the years, Stull Cemetery has developed a reputation far beyond any typical haunted cemetery. Stull Cemetery is said to be the very place where Satan appears to greet his worshipers.

Locals claim that the cemetery is full of demonic forces and despairing specters, and they are not afraid to make their presence known to visitors...

The cemetery itself is on top of a legendary hill called Emmanuel Hill. Stull also hosts a small church and a few resident houses, all of which are perhaps a bit closer to the cemetery than locals would like.

Son of the Devil

Many insidious stories center around Stull Cemetery. The most famous one centers around the spawn of Satan himself.

According to local legend, there was once a boy who lived in Stull who nobody seemed to like. By the age of nine he was estranged from all society and lived on the outskirts of town.

Said to have been born with long red hair and two set of suspiciously pointy teeth, the boy was also known for being incredibly violent towards others. He was cast out by everyone.

As the son of Satan grew up, he learned how to shape shift. He learned how to transform into a dog, a cat and even a wolf. During one of his nightly escapades, a group of villagers hunted the boy down and captured him.

They tied him down in the crawl space of a house. The boy survived on scraps of leftover food that nobody else in the village wanted. Not a lot of time passed before the boy chewed off his own arm in order to escape.

The boy managed to evade the villagers for a total of eleven months after that. During this time period, he became known for sneaking into town and claiming a life. The boy was finally captured by a farmer, and the farmer managed to kill him.

You can guess where his body is buried...

According to other rumors, Stull is also haunted by a witch. This ghostly witch appears as an incredibly tall woman with hair the color of snow. Many warn to never step on the witch's grave or else she will cast an evil spell upon you.

A local group managed to capture several EVP recordings of her, warning them to watch where they stepped.

While these two tales have been passed down through the years, there are more modern accounts of a haunting in Stull Cemetery. In 1974 the University of Kansas covered Stull Cemetery and many strange happenings there, as an article in their school newspaper.

Several students came forward to share their personal accounts of the cemetery. One student swore her arm had been grabbed by an unseen force while there. Another student claimed to have experienced a profound lapse in memory.

Many were convinced that the cemetery belonged to the Devil himself.

Rumors and stories circulated throughout town, and most people agreed that Satan appeared in the cemetery twice each year - once on the Spring Equinox, and then again for Halloween. The cemetery became known for hosting a large group of people twice a year after that.

But when did this haunting truly start?

Some folks believe it goes back all the way to the 1850s...

Satan's Family

During the 1850s, a young stable hand rose to notoriety when he stabbed the mayor while in the barn, which was located on the same grounds as Stull Cemetery. After the crime was committed the barn was torn down, and the land became the construction site of a new church.

During the time of its existence, the church going folk began to notice strange happenings inside the holy building. A large wooden crucifix, which was hung on the wall, was known to turn upside down whenever someone walked near it...

Then shortly after the church was finished, it fell victim to a sudden and mysterious fire.

Many townsfolk believe that Satan visits the cemetery twice a year to see a witch who was buried there. Satan is said to visit her, and to visit his son, whom he created with the witch who still haunts Stull Cemetery. What most visitors find most chilling is the fact that there is indeed a tombstone marked "wittich" located not far from the church.

According to local accounts, the cemetery was once the site of many hangings. An old tree once sat within the cemetery. When the villagers marked a woman as a witch, she would be marched to the cemetery and hung from that tree. Perhaps they had declared their support of Satan before their final moments on earth...

Today, the cemetery has been fenced in, and is heavily guarded by the local police. Those who have visited the cemetery however, have spooky tales of their own. Two men claimed they were exploring in the graveyard at night when a sudden cold gush of wind whirled into them.

Afraid, the two men ran blindly to their car - only to find that the car had moved from where they originally left it. The two eventually found the car, but it was on the opposite side of the highway, facing the wrong direction...

Another man in town also came forward, claiming the same thing had happened to him at Stull as well...

Chapter 11:
Ireland's Gate to the Otherworld

The Ballyboley Forest is located in Larne of Northern Ireland. This dark woods has a nasty reputation that dates back to between the 15th and 17th centuries.

According to legend, during this time period local villagers became known for wandering into the forest but to never appear in town again. Some villagers believed that the forest had once been the home of Druids, while others adhered to Celtic lore and believed the Ballyboley acted as a gateway into the Otherworld.

Today, locals refuse to step foot into this fright-inducing forest. Many claim to have seen strange human-looking entities that wear brown rags. Shadowy animals are also said to meander through the forest at night.

Other villagers report hearing the moans and shrieks of women and trees smeared with blood. No matter if the villagers believe it is a portal or home to shape shifters, most, if not all, agree that the Balleyboley is not to be visited under any circumstances...

Chapter 12:
Death in Love at Dalhousie

In 1247 the Ramsay Clan built a castle called Dalhousie, in Edinburgh, Scotland. The castle remained in the family for 850 years.

During the 16th Century a clanswoman named Catherine Ramsay did something quite scandalous. Rather than aspire to marry one of the nobility, as most of her family did, Catherine fell in love with a servant.

Lady Catherine's parents soon heard of the affair and refused to support it. They demanded that their daughter stop seeing the employee immediately. Heartsick, Lady Catherine found herself wandering through the castle, far away in an upstairs chamber.

She decided to lock herself in and refused to come out or be given food. Lady Catherine slowly died of starvation, still locked in that little room.

Over the centuries, Dalhousie Castle switched hands between rich residents and famous authors. Until 1974, the castle was privately owned. However, that year it was converted into a hotel. Today, the hotel provides unusual and exciting activities, such as falconry. They even offer wedding services.

The Little Girl in Room 4

But amenities and services are not the reason Dalhousie Castle is so popular. Nowadays the hotel attracts attention due to the fact that it is haunted. Several guests have reported terrifying and spooky accounts while staying in the castle...

Several have claimed to have seen the apparition of Lady Catherine herself, roaming the upper chamber, stairs and dungeons while dressed in a formal grey gown.

Helen Parker, a journalist once came to stay in the castle to deliberately interact with the spirits there. While calling out to Lady Catherine, she and her crew could hear a series of knocking on the walls, as if a spirit was trying to communicate in return. She found her time spent at Dalhousie Castle to be the scariest moments of her life.

One family reported that one of the hotel rooms is now haunted by a little girl who was murdered at Dalhousie Castle. A man and his wife booked Room 4 in the castle. His wife felt something stroke her foot, and then they both heard an unseen force gasping from the corner of the room.

When they mentioned the incident to their son, he said he had experienced the same thing while staying in that room on a previous trip.

Some are convinced the hauntings at Dalhousie Castle are real, while others are not convinced. Many locals insist that one night spent at the castle would be enough to convince any skeptic that the spirits are real...

Chapter 13:
The Notorious Waverly Hills

During the late 1800s, tuberculosis was a powerful and deadly disease that spread through the country like wildfire. Once deemed as the White Plague, thousands of people lost their lives to Tuberculosis before a vaccination was discovered.

Before such a medical advance occurred, whole families and towns were wiped out because of this deadly ailment. Louisville, Kentucky was one such place where the population severely dwindled.

In order to save the town, and people's lives, the remaining locals rallied together and built the Waverly Hills Sanatorium in 1926. The hospital was built specifically to house those who were attempting to recover from Tuberculosis.

Despite the state of the art facility, antibiotics were not common during this time period, and hundreds of people still succumbed to the illness while living at Waverly Hills.

At the hospital, all manner of treatments were tried, whether they were comfortable for the patients or not. Some patients were subjected to radiation exposure, or hypothermia from being stranded on open porches during the winter seasons.

When these options did not seem to help a patient, a surgery was often considered. Doctors were known for cutting into a person's chest and placing an inflated balloon within their lungs in an attempt to help them breathe.

This implant, along with the doctor's recommendation to move the ribs around in a way that made breathing easier, were extremely painful and deadly procedures in and of themselves.

Fearful that the townspeople would shut the sanatorium down, they got rid of the bodies of the dead in secret. During construction a chute had been created where a body could be tossed down and sent through a tunnel with tracks. The track ended at the bottom of the hill below the Sanatorium. Bodies were unceremoniously shoved through the chute, and tumbled out at the bottom of the hill in a small pile...

During the 1930s, tuberculosis had died down significantly. When a vaccination was developed and distributed, Waverly Hills had to change gear and cater to new patients with different ailments.

In 1961, the sanatorium was closed down, and reopened a year later as the Woodhaven Geriatrics Sanitarium. Many patients were subjected to electroshock therapy and other barbaric treatments that were popular at the time. However, in less than ten years, the hospital ran out of money. The facility officially closed its doors in 1982.

After that, Waverly Hills passed from owner to owner, however nobody seemed able or willing to revitalize the building into something better. By 2001, Waverly Hills was overrun with homeless people, trash and vandalism. The site has been abandoned for good...

Sure Signs of a Haunting

Considering the number of folks that were mistreated and lost their lives here, it is easy to understand that such a place could be haunted. Waverly Hills has become known for the number of ghosts of children haunting the former hospital.

Some paranormal investigators and other groups have witnessed seeing a little girl, bouncing up and down the stairs to the third floor of the building. Others have reported seeing the spirit of a little boy, playing with an old leather ball.

Many other spirits are also said to haunt Waverly, including a nurse who committed suicide by slicing her wrists open while during a shift at the hospital...

Paranormal investigators who visit the sanatorium often report phantom smells, such as bread baking in the kitchen. They have also reported disembodied voices, footsteps, and doors that slam shut by themselves.

Many of those said groups agree on one thing: the fifth floor has a lot of paranormal activity occurring there. It includes two nurses stations, a linen room, medicine room, pantry and two multi-use rooms as well.

Some have claimed that room 502 is especially haunted, and by a spirit that does not like its privacy being invaded. One group of visitors even heard it order them to get out...

Many people committed suicide in room 502, as a window provided easy access in which to jump out of. A pregnant, unmarried nurse also committed suicide in that room by hanging herself from the light fixture. Visitors have witnessed objects and shadow movements while staying in this room.

Others suggest that the fourth floor is the most haunted floor of the facility. Some visitors believe the floor is home to some unseen presence. As they explored the area, a door slammed nearby, despite the fact that they were alone, and the wind was far too low that day.

That very same group witnessed a full bodied apparition of a doctor appear before one of the guys. The apparition only lasted for a few minutes, but the visitor was very sure of what he had seen.

All in all, there have been far too many paranormal experiences to explain them all away with mere logic. Today, not only is the Waverly Hills Sanatorium an important part of history, but it provides a place for people to experience evidence of the afterlife with their own eyes...

Chapter 14:
The Serial Murders of Franklin Castle

Cleveland, Ohio is home to a very interesting residence, known as Franklin Castle.

Hannes Tiedemann was a local in town. He began his career as a grocer but later made more of a fortune as a banker. After he had made a decent sum of money, Hannes decided to build a large house for himself and his family.

However, after Franklin Castle was built, many unfortunate things began to happen. In 1881, Emma, Hannes' 15 year old daughter died from complications caused by Diabetes. Some folk in town openly disagreed with the prognosis, and claimed they saw poor Emma hanging from her neck up in the attic of the house...

Just a few short weeks later, Hannes' mother also died within the house...

Nobody knew the cause of her death.

From 1886 to 1888 three more of Hannes' children died - none with a reasonable explanation as to why...

Some felt that Hannes' grief took a strange turn when he decided to expand on Franklin Castle following their deaths. He added a ballroom and several rooms that one could only get to by way of secret passages.

In 1895, Hannes wife died in the home as well. While doctors chalked it up to liver disease, many folks in town believed that Hannes had murdered his wife, just as he had murdered everyone else in his family...

But Hannes didn't stop there. His name was often linked with other unsolved murders throughout town. Many believe he had killed a servant girl who was about to marry a local man.

Stricken with jealousy, Hannes killed the girl on her wedding day, along with one of her friends who had witnessed her murder.

In 1906, the last of Hannes' sons died at the age of 42. Two years later Hannes died of a stroke at the age of 75. By then he had no surviving children or family members.

A Dark Mark in History

In 1913, Franklin Castle was purchased by the German Socialist Party, better known as the Nazis. While nobody is exactly sure what took place inside the castle after that, many locals believed Nazi spies were said to be living in the castle.

At least twenty murders occurred in the house during this time. Several doctors were also seen walking in and out of Franklin Castle. Many nearby residents began to suspect that the doctors were performing horrific medical experiments on people within the former home.

The Nazis took advantage of the house's many secret tunnels and passages to hide weaponry and other secret supplies, along with the bodies of murdered victims. Many folks found this horribly ironic, as they believed that the reason Hannes built these secret passages in the first place was so he also could hide bodies inside them...

How Many Bodies?

Today, Franklin Castle is said to be haunted by numerous spirits - the problem is that nobody seems able to identify each spirit because Hannes has been held responsible for so many deaths within the home.

One such sighting is the ghost of a woman, clad all in black. Some speculate the ghost is the servant girl that Hannes killed, while others believe it was one of the many mistresses who met their untimely end in the house. This particular ghost is known to linger by the window turret - where Hannes supposedly chopped her down with an ax...

From 1968 to 1976, the Romano family owned Franklin Castle. One day as they were playing upstairs, the Romano children bounded down the steps and asked their mother if she could provide snacks for their new friend - who was crying upstairs.

When Mrs. Romano went upstairs to check on the supposed child, she couldn't find anybody up there. The family proceeded to experience disembodied footsteps and the sound of an organ being played – however there was no organ in the house!

The Romano family requested that an exorcism be performed on the house, but their request was denied by the Catholic Church. Their local priest did not wish to perform the rite without it being sanctioned, however he did agree that there was an evil presence inside the house.

The Romano family finally decided to move when they were visited by the ghost of a young girl who forewarned them that somebody in the family would die soon. They could no longer handle living in perpetual fear.

During the late 1970s, the Muscatello family bought the house. One day they were shocked to discover a room that had been previously sealed up. When they found a way inside the room they discovered the bones of about a dozen babies...

Nobody could confirm if the bones belonged to Hannes' many children, however the bones were proven to be quite old.

Not long after this discovery, Sam Muscatello became very sick. Desperate for help, he asked a local television station to come and do a story on Franklin Castle. The entire crew was shocked and amazed at the level of paranormal activity they found within the house.

In addition to random cold spots, the crew also heard the phantom sounds of children crying, despite the fact that the Muscatello family didn't have any children.

One local boy claimed he saw the apparition of a woman in white while he was within the house. The spirit glided down the stairs before walking through a closed door.

Visitors have reported seeing the apparition of a young girl in the ballroom of the house. Those who have seen her believe it is the ghost of Hannes' niece, whom he also killed.

Over the next several years, Franklin Castle was passed from owner to owner. Nobody, even those who poured a lot of money into the house, lasted less than a year within its walls. By 1999 four other owners had attempted to live in the house, however nobody felt comfortable enough to do so.

Today, nobody is sure whether or not Hannes actually murdered all of those children and people or not. But many can attest that Franklin Castle is haunted by numerous spirits...

Chapter 15:
The House of the Dead Soldiers

Gettysburg, Pennsylvania is said to be littered with lost souls. Some believe that certain homes within Gettysburg, such as Farnsworth House, are haunted as well. In fact, Farnsworth House has been described as the third most haunted house in all of the United States.

Named after General Farnsworth, who lost his life in the Battle of Gettysburg, the house was built in the early 19th Century. The house became the local home of Confederate soldiers during the American Civil War.

Two decades after it was completed, the house was sold to a man named John McFarland. John took it upon himself to add an additional 3.5 stories to the house, constructed all in brick. The home started to resemble the layout and architectural design of a fortress.

During the Civil War, the Confederacy stumbled upon the house and thought it would be ideal for sharpshooters. They were only about one hundred yards from where Union soldiers lurked behind a hill.

During this time the house was home to the Sweeny family, however they had retreated to a place of safety during the three-day battle of Gettysburg.

When the Union won the Civil War, numerous Union soldiers used the house until the Sweeny family returned to reclaim their property.

Much later in the house's history, Farnsworth was converted into a bed and breakfast. It already had five guestrooms, but five more were added. Today, Farnsworth continues to operate as a bed and breakfast, and caters to Civil War buffs who wish to purchase memorabilia and view the battlefield.

Those who operate Farnsworth House accept that the house comes with a number of spirits. They offer a ghost tour to anyone who desires to learn more about the hauntings on site. Guests are recommended to request a haunted or non-haunted room during their stay, in order for everyone to have an ideal vacation according to their needs and desires.

The Young Ghosts

Some of the Farnsworth rooms are more popular than others. For example, the Sarah Black room is among their most popular. Sarah was the daughter of George and Verna, the first couple to convert Farnsworth House into a bed and breakfast.

In this room it is rumored that the ghost of a little boy is said to appear. The boy is said to be named Jeremy. According to local legend, Jeremy was run over by a horse and carriage while playing with his friends on the property. He was taken into the now famous room to await a doctor.

While the doctor examined Jeremy, his father is said to have paced outside the door, demanding an update while he pounded on the door frame. Today, brave souls who request this room will often hear the sound of a phantom fist, banging against their door during the night.

Some guests have been known to bring toys to give to Jeremy. His ghost is known for stealing precious items he finds in the room, and said items will only be returned in exchange for a toy...

Those who do not witness Jeremy are often visited by another ghost, this time in the shape of a midwife named Mary. Mary's job was to attend to the ill who lived within the house. Visitors are more likely to see Mary if they are ill during their stay at Farnsworth House.

Known as a warm, and non-scary ghost, Mary can be seen hovering over a person's bed, stroking their hair in a soothing fashion.

In the kitchen another spirit resides. Staff have reported seeing the ghost of an old woman dressed in a gown from the 19th Century. This ghost is said to appear out of a cloud of black mist, and check to see that the kitchen is well stocked with supplies. The spirit will disappear if anybody attempts to approach her.

A few guests have reported seeing ghostly soldiers up in the attic of the house. The soldiers are said to be "on duty" as they peer out from the attic windows, on the lookout for Union soldiers. When one was shot, their body was pushed to the other side of the attic while the battle continued. Many wound up dying up in the small room.

When the spirits begin to die down each night, eerie sounds and voices can be heard traveling through Farnsworth House. Some claim to have heard the sounds of a Jew harp, while others report hearing the sounds of singing from an unseen source.

Often the soldiers would sing while carrying dead comrades down to the basement of the house, to be stored until burial.

A few years ago, a radio station in the area decided to record their Halloween show from within Farnsworth House. The group happened to be dressed all in blue as they began to set up their various equipment in the house.

Apparently being surrounded by so much blue made the ghostly soldiers quite active. They could be heard whispering and shuffling about the place. When a medium was brought in, she said she felt their distress very easily. When she asked what was wrong, one of the soldiers replied that there were Union soldiers in the house, and they did not want their cover blown...

Chapter 16:
The Infamous Bell Witch Attack

Now a famous house, the story of the Bell Witch begins in 1804. The Bell family, which consisted of John, his wife and their six children, moved to Red River, Tennessee from their previous residence in North Carolina.

John Bell purchased a respectable plot of land and a comfortable house. Over the next couple of years, John continued to purchase more property, until their land consisted of 300 acres. After they had settled in, the Bells had three more children in the house.

Nearly ten years later it is said that John Bell was out amongst his crops when he came across a most peculiar animal. The animal was said to have the head of a rabbit and the body of a dog. John attempted to shoot the animal down, but it disappeared before he could get a good shot at it.

After that, strange things began to take place in the Bell home. Loud noises and clanks could be heard emanating from outside the house during the darkest hours of the night. No matter how prepared John and his sons were to capture the strange beast, they never saw anything the moment they ran outside...

As this persisted, the young children in the family began to complain that something was rapidly moving underneath their beds at night. When John claimed it was nothing but mice, chewing on the wood, things quickly escalated.

The children began to cry, and tell their parents that something was stealing their blankets and pillows at night. The spirit could then be heard whispering to the family from underneath the beds. Betsy, the youngest of all the siblings seemed most prone to attacks by the spirit.

It became routine for the ghost to pull at Betsy's hair and slap her across the face without warning. The Bells were desperate for help and support from the community. They asked their friends, the Johnstons, to stay the night at their house one night and experience the haunting for themselves.

It didn't take long for Mrs. Johnston to become the subject of harsh slaps. James Johnston confronted the ghost, and it disappeared - but only for that night.

As the haunting escalated, General Jackson caught wind of the trouble, and decided to help the Bell family, as they had served their country under the general during the battle of New Orleans. General Jackson assembled a group of men and traveled to Red River by way of a horse drawn carriage.

And yet when the carriage arrived on the property, the horses refused to take another step. They neighed nervously, and pawed at the ground in uncertainty. The General began to shout that it was the witch's doing - and the witch admitted that it was...

During that night, General Jackson and his troop fell victim to repeated, harsh beatings and torment by the witch. The following morning, they quickly assembled their gear and left the property, wholly convinced that something paranormal lived there, and that there was no way they could help the Bell family.

As Betsy grew, the entity grew quite attached to the young woman. When the Bell's neighbor, Joshua Gardner asked for Betsy's hand in marriage everyone was ecstatic at the news - except for the witch.

The spirit began to stalk the pair and would often cause them to argue. Fed up, Joshua broke off the engagement to Betsy.

Soon after John Bell became quite ill. He suffered many stroke-like symptoms and seemed in constant shortness of breath. Right after he died the family found a strange vial of liquid amongst his medications. When they fed the remaining contents of the vial to the family cat, the cat died within minutes...

Horrified, the Bells cast the vial into the fire, and the witch's voice could be heard telling them that she had poisoned John Bell. After that, the witch came and went as it pleased. Each time the witch would tell the family she would be back at a certain point in time, and she always reappeared without fail.

In 1828, the witch visited John Junior. She is said to have had many conversations with him about war, humanity and Christianity. After that she said she would reappear to the Bell family 107 years later. She did so to Charles Bailey Bell, who wound up writing a book about the witch in 1934.

Today, nobody is entirely sure who the Bell Witch really was. Some believed it was a neighbor who hated John Bell and wanted to get back at him. Others thought it was the machinations of the local school teacher Richard Powell, who was smitten with Betsy.

After the death of Joshua, Betsy agreed to marry Richard. His wife had died earlier that year, due to unknown causes.

The Bell house and the Bell Witch Cave are available to tour now. Many warn not to take a rock from the infamous cave, because the witch will haunt you and curse you until you send it back to the cave.

Some people are convinced they wound up in the hospital with horrible illnesses, all thanks to the Bell Witch. Unfortunately, we may never know who she really was, and whether or not she was the result of an elaborate hoax, or the manifestation of evil in human form...

Chapter 17:
The Romanian Bermuda Triangle

Considered to be the most haunted forest in the entire world, the Hoia Baciu Forest is located west of Cluj-Napoca, Romania. This forest is called the Bermuda Triangle of Romania by the locals.

Centuries ago, Romanians used the forest as a place to kill off peasants within the community. Locals believe that the souls of those peasants are what first made the Hoia haunted.

This vast and thick forest is said to be haunted by many misty apparitions and not to mention several Unidentified Flying Objects.

Those who have visited this forest have all described an uneasy anxiety take over their bodies while they were within the forest. Many claimed they felt as though they were being watched at all times as they migrated through the dense foliage. Nausea, throwing up, headaches, and scratches have all been reported by visitors who explore the forest.

Even the origin of the forest's name has a creepy story behind it. The woods are named after a shepherd who is said to have entered the woods along with 200 sheep. But neither the man or his sheep, ever reappeared from the depths of the trees.

After his mysterious disappearance, the forest developed a sinister reputation in town. Many townsfolk refused to go near it, thinking it was an evil place. Some were convinced that while they did not think a spirit would haunt them, they believed they would not able to find their way back once they traveled within its borders.

The Hoia Baciu gained national attention during the 1960s, when a man named Alexander Sift took what is supposedly photographic evidence of a UFO flying over the forest. In 1968 Emil Barnea also took a picture of a flying saucer hovering over the tree line. From that point on, the Hoia became a popular destination for tourists who wished to see a flying saucer.

For most visitors, their trip can be described in much the same fashion... devices, such as GPS and cellphones do not seem to work well within the forest - they have a tendency to malfunction at random.

Visitors report hearing disembodied female voices and giggles surrounding them while in the forest. And most will report feeling physical symptoms, such as rashes, feeling light headed and otherwise quite ill.

Some locals have become convinced that not only is the Hoia Baciu haunted, but it also provides some form of gateway into another dimension - hence why equipment malfunctions and many UFOs have been spotted within the area.

A couple of visitors back up this theory by explaining that they lost all manner of time while exploring the forest. A few of them found themselves traveling outside the forest, but could not recall the steps they took in leaving it.

One of the most famous stories about the forest is the tale of a little girl who once got lost in the dense forest. She did not reappear again for another five years. She wore the same clothes she had disappeared in, but had no recollection of anything that happened after she slipped behind the border of trees.

Camping Gone Wrong

A group of friends decided to explore the forest. They wanted to take their time, so they planned to camp overnight. It rained heavily as they decided to call it a night. They assembled makeshift tents made out of hammocks.

When the sun rose the following morning, the group were horrified and shocked to discover that one of the group members started speaking in tongues.

Some of the group members argued that the man in question was known for talking in his sleep. However, they also admitted that he had never spoken in another language before!

All in all, most people try to avoid the Hoia Baciu forest at all costs in their day to day life. Those who travel across the globe to visit it can attest that the forest is a crazy place, filled with a heaviness that you can't escape from. Nobody who enters the forest is the same when they leave it – that's if they ever do...

Chapter 18:
The Haunted Rock of the Night

Craig-y-Nos (which translates to "rock of the night") is a castle located in the Upper Swansea Valley in Wales. Used today as a boutique hotel, the castle has had three private owners: The Powell family, the Morgan family and then the opera singer, Adelina Patti.

The castle was built, brick by brick in 1841, and was completed in 1843. The Powell family designed it and moved in, but quickly died off. Captain Powell believed his family was cursed through their ancient Dutch bloodlines.

By 1864, the Powell family had all but died out. Sarah Powell was the inheritor, and moved in with her husband. However, her husband passed away in 1875, and Sarah decided to sell the castle once and for all.

Craig-y-Nos wound up in the hands of Morgan Morgan and his family. Mr. Morgan had purchased the estate for 6,000 pounds. The family stayed in the house for two years before they sold the property to Adelina Patti...

The House of the Opera Singer

It is said that Adelina fell in love with the castle the moment she set eyes on it. After she purchased it, she rarely left the house - only to perform and tour the United States.

Adelina decided to marry for the second time. She married singer Ernesto Nicolini. After the ceremony, Adelina decided to remodel the house, one room at a time.

In 1914, Adelina retired from performing and remained in the castle for the rest of her days. She passed away in 1919.

In 1921, Craig-y-Nos was converted into a temporary hospital to handle the outbreak of Tuberculosis. It remained a hospital until 1986.

A Most Haunted Hotel

In the year 2000, the castle was purchased and converted into a hotel. Some believe the hauntings began when the castle was converted for the hotel industry. However, many nurses can attest that the hauntings began back when the castle was used as a hospital...

Several nurses reported seeing a strange and blurry figure walk by them during their usual rounds. Others have been terrified to see black shadows lingering in the corners of some of the rooms. A few even reported hearing disembodied noises throughout certain parts of the hospital.

Many locals are convinced that in addition to the spirits of dead tuberculosis patients, the house is also haunted by Adelina herself, in addition to her second husband, Ernesto.

Occasionally the castle is used for media purposes. Once a local film crew was there, shooting scenes for an upcoming movie. According to rumors, when one of the crew members began to speak of Adelina, and her inability to successfully complete a certain task, a saucepan fell off the counter and onto the floor.

Many staff members insisted that Adelina had done it, as a matter of showing that she was angry at receiving such criticism...

It would seem that certain parts of the castle are more haunted than others. For example the Conservatory is said to be quite active. When Craig-y-Nos was used as a hospital this section of the house was used for the children. Many of them unfortunately perished within that room. Their spirits are said to remain there, laughing and crying...

The Breakfast Room, which happened to be Adelina's favorite part of the house, is also said to be quite active. Many visitors report a presence in that room that is impossible to ignore.

A few unlucky guests reported feeling molested by an unseen phantom while exploring the cellar of the house. Nobody is quite sure whether the spirit died in the castle when it was a hospital, or if it had been a member of Adelina's staff prior to that.

But of all the rooms and quarters within the castle, Room 36 is believed to be the most haunted of all. According to some of the brave souls who have elected to stay in that room during their stay, the room is known for playing crazy tricks on residents.

One man woke up in the middle of the night to find a door that hadn't been there when he had gone to bed. He claimed that a woman was seen sitting on the edge of his bed. After a few moments, the ghost rose up and walked through the door, where a chapel had once been.

Dave Cottle, a musician, claims to have had a surreal experience while at Craig-y-Nos. Dave claimed to have conversed with a spirit while sitting at the hotel bar. A woman, dressed all in the black, approached him and asked if he was a singer.

Dave explained that he was a musician and that he didn't sing. When two of his band mates approached, they asked Dave who he was speaking to. They could not see the woman in black, seated beside him...

What had been previously used as a theater was converted into a playroom for the children during the castle's time as a hospital. Now the room is believed to be haunted by ghost children. A phantom ball can often be heard being bounced around on the floor and walls of the room. Several visitors have reported hearing this ball on multiple occasions.

The owner of the castle, a man named Martin, has had his own fair share of experiences at the castle, but none as vivid as the door by the Patti Bar. Martin and a cook were in the kitchen preparing food when the door began to move backwards and forwards at an alarming speed.

As Martin and the chef watched the door, both were immediately convinced that it was not the act of a human. No human could have manipulated the door with such speed in such a short amount of time. The incident was incredibly unnerving as neither of them could explain how the door moved when nobody else was around and all the windows had been closed...

Even animals have sensed a paranormal entity within the castle. One man toured the facility with several other business owners. The man had his dog accompany them on tour. All of a sudden the dog stopped dead in his tracks and refused to go any further. He started to bark and work himself up into a frenzy, staring at something nobody else in the group could see.

The staff members were convinced the dog had picked up on the haunting, and was reacting to it...

Conclusion

It takes a very simple, but very dark formula for a location, be it a house, hospital or even forest, to become haunted. All of the places discussed in the book have one thing in common: many souls have died in each location prior to the beginning of paranormal activity being reported.

While benign hauntings do occasionally happen - such as Adelina Patti haunting the castle because she loved the place so dearly - most hauntings are the cause of a tragic or violent event in history.

Children who succumb to illness before they have a chance to really experience life...

Cousins, nieces and distant relations being brutally murdered within the comfort of their own home...

Depressed individuals in search of a place to end their own lives...

The various locations in this book are all haunted because the location became the spot of an untimely or intense death. These environments have absorbed the negative emotions of these events and retained them within their very roots, within their very walls.

Now these residual hauntings are viewed by curious visitors from all over the world. These ghosts, ghouls and misty apparitions provide evidence of another world we may get to pass into when we die. A world we have no way of understanding until we have crossed over ourselves.

Many paranormal investigators are convinced that these spirits wish to interact with the living, for the most part. By use of electromagnetic energy found in devices, spirits are able to gather power and reach out to us, by way of voice, sound, or a specific bodily form.

And such hauntings have been caught and recorded by many groups of people over a long period of time.

Sometimes these experiences can be terrifying. After all, not every spirit that has crossed over to the other side is pleasant - or even aware of their own death. But despite the terror of the unknown, and of the dead, finding haunted places such as these provides some strange semblance of comfort.

Life does not end when we exhale our last breath in this world. Our journey will only continue...

If you enjoyed this book, do you think you could leave me a review on Amazon? Just search for this title and my name on Amazon to find it. Thank you so much, it is very much appreciated!

Other Books Written By Me

Below you'll find some of my other popular books that are popular on Amazon and Kindle as well. You can visit my author page on Amazon to see other work done by me. (Max Mason Hunter).

Unexplained Phenomena

Unexplained Phenomena – Book 2

Bizarre True Stories

True Paranormal

True Paranormal – Book 2

True Paranormal – Book 3

True Ghost Stories And Hauntings

True Ghost Stories And Hauntings – Book 2

True Ghost Stories And Hauntings – Book 3

True Paranormal Hauntings

True Paranormal Hauntings – Book 2

True Paranormal Hauntings – Book 3

True Paranormal Hauntings – Book 4

Ghost Stories

You can simply search for these titles on the Amazon website with my name to find them.

LIBRARY BUGS BOOKS

Like books?

Would you like them delivered to you every week?

Do you like non-fiction books on a huge range of different topics?

We send out e-books every week so we can share our books with the world!

We have books every week on AMAZON that we send to our email list. If you want in, then visit the link below to sign up and sit back and wait for new books to be sent straight to your inbox!

It couldn't be simpler!

www.LibraryBugs.com

If you want books delivered straight to your inbox, then visit the link above and soon you'll be receiving a great list of e-books every week!

Enjoy :)